THE STORY OF THE
**OAKLAND
ATHLETICS**

Published by Creative Education
P.O. Box 227, Mankato, Minnesota 56002
Creative Education is an imprint of The Creative Company

Design and production by Blue Design
Printed in the United States of America

Photographs by Corbis (Underwood & Underwood), Getty Images (Jeff Carlick/MLB Photos, Alfred Eisenstaedt//Time
Life Pictures, Focus on Sport, Otto Greule Jr, Otto Greule Jr/Allsport, Hulton Archive, Jed Jacobsohn, Francis Miller//Time
Life Pictures, National Baseball Hall of Fame Library/MLB Photos, New York Times Co., Doug Pensinger, Mark Rucker/
Transcendental Graphics, Herb Scharfman/Sports Imagery, Don Smith/MLB Photos, Jamie Squire/Allsport, Tony Tomsic,
Tony Tomsic/MLB Photos, Michael Zagaris)

Library of Congress Cataloging-in-Publication Data

Pueschner, Gordon.
The story of the Oakland Athletics / by Gordon Pueschner.
p. cm. — (Baseball: the great American game)
Includes index.
ISBN-13: 978-1-58341-496-5
1. Oakland Athletics (Baseball team)—History—Juvenile literature. I. Title. II. Series.

GV875.O24P84 2007
796.357'640979466—dc22   2006027453

First Edition
9 8 7 6 5 4 3 2 1

Cover: Outfielder Rickey Henderson
Page 1: Pitcher Chief Bender
Page 3: Shortstop Bobby Crosby

THE STORY OF THE
OAKLAND ATHLETICS

by Gordon Pueschner

GENE TENACE

Oakland Athletics

When he stepped up to the plate in Game 1 of the 1972 World Series, Oakland Athletics catcher Gene Tenace didn't know that this would be the day he made it into the record books, becoming the first player in World Series history to hit home runs in his first two at bats. Because teammate Reggie Jackson had been sidelined by an injury in the last playoff game, Tenace, who had hit only five homers during the season, was bumped into the rotation in the slugger's place. It was the right move. His two home runs brought in three runs and a win for Oakland that first game. Tenace

went on to hit two more home runs and collect nine runs batted in throughout the next six games, earning series Most Valuable Player honors for his role in propelling the Athletics to their first World Series title in 42 years.

THE FIRST DYNASTY

O akland, California, sits on the eastern edge of San Francisco Bay. It was originally founded in 1820, but the town didn't boom until 1852, when the gold rush brought thousands of wealth-seekers to California. Today, Oakland is a sprawling metropolis of nearly 400,000 people. The busy city manufactures canvas, electronics, and metal products, and is home to the Port of Oakland, one of the largest shipping ports on America's West Coast.

The history of Oakland's professional baseball team, the Athletics, goes all the way back to 1893 and halfway across the country, where the team originated as the Indianapolis Indians, a minor-league club that was part of the Western League. In 1901, the team moved to Philadelphia to become a charter member of the newly-formed American League (AL). Former catcher Connie Mack was chosen to manage what was then called the Philadelphia Athletics—a team he would own and manage for the next 50 years.

In the team's second year, six batters hit over .300 to help Philadelphia win its first AL pennant. The Athletics won it again in 1905 and advanced to their first-ever World Series, where the New York Giants trampled them. The Athletics returned to the World Series in 1910 to face the heavily favored

FRANK BAKER

Early Philadelphia star Frank "Home Run" Baker gave the Athletics rare long-ball power for seven seasons.

Nicknamed "The Tall Tactician," Connie Mack was known for his dignified manner and steady success.

Chicago Cubs, baseball's first dynasty, who were appearing in their fourth World Series in five years. Using only two pitchers, Jack Coombs and Charles "Chief" Bender, in the five-game series, the Athletics defeated the Cubs and claimed their first World Series title.

Philadelphia continued its dominance in 1911, winning the AL pennant behind the arm of pitcher Eddie Plank, who won 23 games with a sidearm curveball and a painfully slow delivery that frustrated batters. Sportswriter David Pietrusza noted that "the deliberate Plank would stand on the mound and rub up the baseball, adjust his belt, step off the mound, knock dirt from his spikes, go back to the mound and ask for a new sign, reposition his cap, pull up a sock, and finally throw a pitch."

CHIEF BENDER – A member of the Chippewa tribe, Bender faced discrimination even as he became one of baseball's best pitchers. He was known for a special pitch that was part fastball and part curveball, and his "nickel curve" helped him win 212 career games.

CHIEF BENDER

PITCHER · LEFTY GROVE

During his time in Philadelphia, Robert Moses "Lefty" Grove racked up an astonishing 195–79 record, with seven consecutive seasons of 20 or more wins. He was so dominant in one 1929 game against the Yankees that—with a one-run lead, no outs, and one player on base—he struck out New York legends Babe Ruth, Lou Gehrig, and Bob Meusel in 10 pitches. Grove also had a destructive temper, sometimes shredding his uniform or ripping apart lockers after a loss. But wins were much more common. He posted a 300–141 career record and a .680 winning percentage, the highest of any major-league pitcher with that many games.

LEFTY GROVE
PITCHER

OAKLAND
ATHLETICS

STATS

Athletics seasons: 1925–33

Height: 6-2

Weight: 190

- **9-time AL leader in ERA**
- **6-time All-Star**
- **1931 AL MVP**
- **Baseball Hall of Fame inductee (1947)**

THE WHITE ELEPHANT

In 1901, Connie Mack and his Philadelphia Athletics were part of the upstart AL. Many members of the National League (NL), including New York Giants manager John McGraw, didn't appreciate the addition of the new league. McGraw thought the A's wouldn't be able to compete. He even jokingly began calling the A's the "White Elephants," in reference to the large amounts of money Mack was putting into a ballclub McGraw believed would fall on its face. Shortly thereafter, Mack defiantly adopted the white elephant as the team's symbol in hopes of spurring his team to greatness. It seemed to work: in 1902, the A's went on to win the AL pennant, and in 1905, they played in the World Series (which was founded in 1903). The white elephant wouldn't become the team's official mascot until 1918, when it was finally placed on the sleeve of the uniform. Two years later, the elephant made it onto the front of the uniform but would come and go for the next 60 years until 1988, when it was brought back for good. Not only has it proven to be a good luck charm, but it has become one of baseball's most familiar and successful team insignias.

The Athletics faced their old nemesis, the New York Giants, in the World Series that year. Philadelphia lost a close Game 1 but bounced back in Game 2 with Plank's help, winning 3–1. The Athletics claimed the next two games and were about to close out the series when the Giants rallied in the 10th inning to win Game 5. But it wouldn't matter in the end, as the Athletics rolled over them 13–2 in Game 6 to capture their second World Series in a row. Philadelphia continued its dominance by winning another world championship in 1913 and was favored to beat the underdog Boston Braves in the 1914 World Series. But it was not to be. Despite the great play of star third baseman Frank Baker, the Athletics were swept in four games, and their stranglehold on major league baseball was officially broken.

The Athletics' first dynasty came to an end the following year, as the team dropped to last place with a staggering 109 losses. The decline was due in part to the new Federal League, which lured many of Connie Mack's best players away with bigger contracts. Mack refused to match the salaries, and the team suffered the consequences as such stars as Plank and Bender left. In 1916, the Athletics hit a league low, going 36–117. Philadelphia would remain near the bottom of the league for the next 10 years.

CATCHER · MICKEY COCHRANE

On April 14, 1925, Mickey Cochrane made his major-league debut along with pitcher Lefty Grove. It marked the only time two future Hall-of-Famers ever started their careers in the same game. Cochrane hit .331 in his first year, the first of nine total .300 seasons. His hitting ability helped the A's reach the World Series in 1929, 1930, and 1931, but his playing days ended when he was hit in the head by a pitch in 1937. Cochrane was unconscious for 10 days and wasn't expected to survive. Against all odds, he finally recovered but never played baseball again.

STATS

Athletics seasons: 1925–33

Height: 5-10

Weight: 180

- **2-time All-Star**

- **2-time AL MVP**

- **.320 career BA**

- **Baseball Hall of Fame inductee (1947)**

MICKEY COCHRANE
CATCHER

OAKLAND
ATHLETICS

From 1929 to 1935, offensive powerhouse
Jimmie Foxx (left) averaged 138 RBI and
122 runs scored per season.

JIMMIE FOXX

CONNIE'S BULL ELEPHANTS

onnie Mack rebuilt the team in the mid-1920s around a new batch of talented players, among them future Hall of Fame first baseman Jimmie Foxx. Because of his ability to hit the long ball, people started referring to Foxx as "the right-handed Babe Ruth." Foxx's strength was so overwhelming that New York Yankees hurler Lefty Gomez once said, "I was pitching one day when my glasses clouded up on me. I took them off to polish them. When I looked up to the plate, I saw Jimmie Foxx. The sight of him terrified me so much that I haven't been able to wear glasses since."

In 1927 and 1928, the Athletics finished in second place in the AL behind the mighty Yankees, and from 1929 to 1931, the league's premier pitching duo, Athletics stars Lefty Grove and George "The Moose" Earnshaw, won a combined 146 games. In 1929, everything came together, and the Athletics won the AL pennant. Once again, they found themselves facing the Cubs in the World Series, and once again, they defeated them four games to one. The Athletics locked up another World Series trophy the following year by defeating the St. Louis Cardinals and became the first team ever to win two back-to-back world championships.

THE 1929 A'S

The 1929 Athletics are considered by many baseball experts to be the finest team in history. That year, the A's went 104–46 and captured Philadelphia's first AL pennant in 15 years. Philadelphia's lineup had five regulars batting above .300, including center fielder Al Simmons (157 runs batted in, or RBI), first baseman Jimmie Foxx (33 home runs), and outfielder Bing Miller (183 hits). The Athletics' pitching staff recorded the lowest earned run average (ERA) in the AL and also boasted two 20-game winners—George Earnshaw and Lefty Grove. In Game 1 of the World Series against the Chicago Cubs, Connie Mack surprised everyone by starting the team's seventh-best pitcher, Howard Ehmke, who ended up setting a World Series record with 13 strikeouts and won the game 3–1. Earnshaw won Game 2, but the Cubs snatched Game 3 away from him in their only series win. In Game 4, the A's bounced back from an 8–3 deficit with help from Simmons, Foxx, and infielder Jimmy Dykes, who scored the go-ahead run to top Chicago 10–8. A Miller home run that bounced off the scoreboard in Game 5 sealed the deal, and the A's captured their fourth World Series title.

"Connie's Bull Elephants," as many called them, trounced the competition in 1931, winning a franchise-record 107 games and another pennant. The team boasted six future Hall-of-Famers, including Grove, who won an astounding 31 games. Teammate and outfielder Doc Cramer explained this phenomenon: "He didn't have a curve—all he had was a fastball. Everybody knew what they were going to hit at, but they still couldn't hit him." On the offensive side, 37-year-old outfielder Bing "Old Reliable" Miller continued to be known for his timely hitting and led the club in doubles, with 43.

The Athletics faced the Cardinals in the 1931 World Series for a chance to become baseball's first "three-peat." Grove threw a victorious 6–2 series opener, but Philadelphia was blanked in Game 2, and it came up short again in Game 3. Down but not out, Mack's Athletics came back in Game 4 behind Earnshaw's two-hit triumph. The teams split the next two games, leaving the series tied 3–3. The final contest did not start well for the Athletics, as a wild pitch and an error helped the Cardinals take a two-run lead. The Athletics rallied in the ninth but ultimately came up short, losing 4–2.

After that, Philadelphia started to slide down in the standings, finishing 1932 in second place and 1933 in third. Faced with financial problems due to the Great Depression and decreased attendance at games, Mack once again

FIRST BASEMAN · JIMMIE FOXX

Foxx, a farm boy from Maryland, grew up doing chores, giving him the build that would one day allow him to hit 534 home runs. He was such a fearsome hitter that fans called him "The Beast," and he crushed 30 or more home runs in 12 consecutive seasons. Foxx was so powerful that he once hit a ball over the double-decker stands in Chicago's Comiskey Park, even clearing the adjoining 34th Street. In the 1935 All-Star Game in Cleveland, the longtime Philadelphia star hit a home run into the upper deck, breaking one of the stadium's seats.

STATS

Athletics seasons: 1925–35

Height: 6-0

Weight: 195

- **534 career HR**
- **9-time All-Star**
- **3-time AL MVP**
- **Baseball Hall of Fame inductee (1951)**

JIMMIE FOXX
FIRST BASEMAN

OAKLAND ATHLETICS

needed to make money, so he sold clutch-hitting outfielder Al Simmons to the Chicago White Sox and Grove to the Boston Red Sox. His top talent gone, Mack's Athletics hit rock bottom in 1935 and would linger there for the next 34 years, never rising higher than fourth place in the AL.

AL SIMMONS – One of Connie Mack's favorite and most reliable players, Simmons was called "Bucketfoot Al" due to the way he stepped toward the dugout when swinging. He was the AL batting champion in both 1930 and 1931, putting up .381 and .390 averages.

THE SWINGIN' A'S

In 1950, after 50 years of coaching the Athletics, 88-year-old Connie Mack finally retired, but his team continued to falter. Attendance and revenue plummeted throughout the '50s until Chicago businessman Arnold Johnson took ownership and moved the Athletics to Kansas City in 1954. Their new hometown fans were eager to support the struggling team, turning out in record numbers that first year: 1,393,054 people flocked to Kansas City Municipal Stadium in 1955 to see what the team had to offer. It wasn't much; the Athletics finished last or next-to-last for each of the next six seasons.

Insurance tycoon Charlie O. Finley bought the team in 1960 and quickly made his purpose known. "My intentions are to keep the Athletics permanently in Kansas City and build a winning ballclub," he announced. Finley did develop a minor-league system that would help the Athletics recruit talent, but despite his outward promises to never relocate, "Charlie O." spent more time and money shopping the club around the league during the next seven years than he did on quality players. In 1967, Finley was finally granted permission to move the Athletics to Oakland, California.

Owner Charlie O. Finley was known for his wacky promotional techniques and frequent quarrels with players.

CHARLIE O. FINLEY

The change of scenery worked this time; the 1968 Athletics, now commonly known as the A's, finished with a winning record (82–80). All-Star shortstop Bert Campaneris led Oakland in hits, runs, and triples that year; future stars such as third baseman Sal Bando and pitcher Rollie Fingers came on board; and pitcher Jim "Catfish" Hunter threw the AL's first regular-season perfect game in 46 years against the Minnesota Twins. "It has to be one of my biggest thrills in baseball, right up there with winning a World Series game," Hunter said of the feat.

The next year, when the AL was divided into two divisions (the A's going into the AL Western Division), Oakland finished in second place, but the real story in 1969 was second-year sensation Reggie Jackson, who hit 47 home runs and became a fan favorite wherever he played. In 1971, the outfielder swatted 32 homers, helping "The Swingin' A's" seize the AL West. In the playoffs, though, they lost to the Baltimore Orioles, who would go on to win the 1971 World Series.

Oakland rebounded in 1972, storming to the top of its division and defeating the Detroit Tigers in the AL Championship Series (ALCS) to make its first appearance in a World Series in 41 years. When Jackson was injured during the last game of the ALCS, fans wondered whether their underdog

SECOND BASEMAN · MAX BISHOP

Max Bishop was regarded as one of the best fielders in the major leagues during his time, but the quiet and unassuming second baseman earned the nickname "Camera Eye" because of his uncanny knowledge of the strike zone. Six times in 12 seasons, he accumulated more bases on balls than hits, twice drawing five walks in a single game. As fellow A's infielder Jimmie Dykes explained, "Max had one of the greatest batting eyes in the game. If he didn't swing at a pitch, the umpires just assumed that it didn't catch the plate and called it a ball."

MAX BISHOP
SECOND BASEMAN

OAKLAND
ATHLETICS

STATS

Athletics seasons: 1924–31

Height: 5-8

Weight: 165

- **.271 career BA**
- **379 career RBI**
- **4-time AL leader in fielding percentage**
- **Career-high 128 walks in 1929**

THIRD BASEMAN · SAL BANDO

Sal Bando's .254 career batting average may not seem impressive, but he was considered by many as the glue that held the "Swingin' A's" together in the 1970s. He was co-captain of the Oakland team that won five straight AL West titles. His best year by far was 1973, when he slugged 29 home runs, slapped 32 doubles, and posted 98 RBI. In the second game of the 1973 ALCS against the Baltimore Orioles, he blasted two home runs in a 6–3 win. He also had the honor of hitting Oakland's first grand slam on April 16, 1969.

SAL BANDO
THIRD BASEMAN

OAKLAND
ATHLETICS

STATS

Athletics seasons: 1966–76

Height: 6-0

Weight: 205

- **.254 career BA**

- **1,039 career RBI**

- **1973 AL leader in doubles (32)**

- **4-time All-Star**

IMPROBABLE VICTORY

Oakland limped into the 1972 World Series against the Cincinnati Reds without its two key players, right fielder Reggie Jackson and pitcher Darold Knowles. The Reds, led by outfielder Pete Rose, were confident and highly favored to win. If the A's were to overcome the odds, it was going to take a team effort, and the first to step up was back-up utility catcher Gene Tenace, who had gone a meager 1-for-17 in the playoffs. But in Game 1 alone, he hit two home runs in his first two at bats (a World Series record) and helped the A's take the game 3–1. Oakland outfielder Joe Rudi became the hero of

Game 2 when he hit a home run and made an amazing game-saving catch. The A's lost Game 3, but in Game 4, after trailing 2–1, shortstop Gonzalo Marquez, Tenace, and outfielder Angel Mangual nailed consecutive singles to win the game. Although Games 5 and 6 went to the Reds, the A's weren't ready to give up yet. Game 7 was played back in Cincinnati's hostile Riverfront Stadium, and Tenace again drove in two runs and led the team to an improbable 3–2 victory, making the A's world champions for the first time in 42 years.

A's would be able to withstand the "Big Red Machine" of the Cincinnati Reds in the World Series. They didn't have to worry, as an unlikely hero arrived in the form of quiet catcher Gene Tenace. His four home runs and nine RBI during Oakland's four-games-to-three victory over Cincinnati made up for Jackson's absence and powered the A's to their sixth world championship. "It's hard to explain how those things happen," said a mystified Tenace afterward. "I was kind of in a zone mentally, and every pitch I saw . . . looked down the middle to me."

The entire Oakland team was in the zone the next season, as closer Rollie Fingers earned 22 saves and won 7 games to help the A's march to another AL West title. They then defeated the Orioles in the ALCS and went on to face the New York Mets in the World Series. In the bottom of the third inning in Game 7, Campaneris and Jackson each hit a home run, knocking in a total of four runs. Oakland never gave up its lead and cruised to its seventh World Series victory.

The mighty A's coasted to the World Series again in 1974, this time meeting the Los Angeles Dodgers, and tried once again to win a third straight World Series. The A's and Dodgers split the first two games, but Fingers saved Games 3, 4, and 5 for Oakland, earning the series Most Valuable Player

CATFISH HUNTER

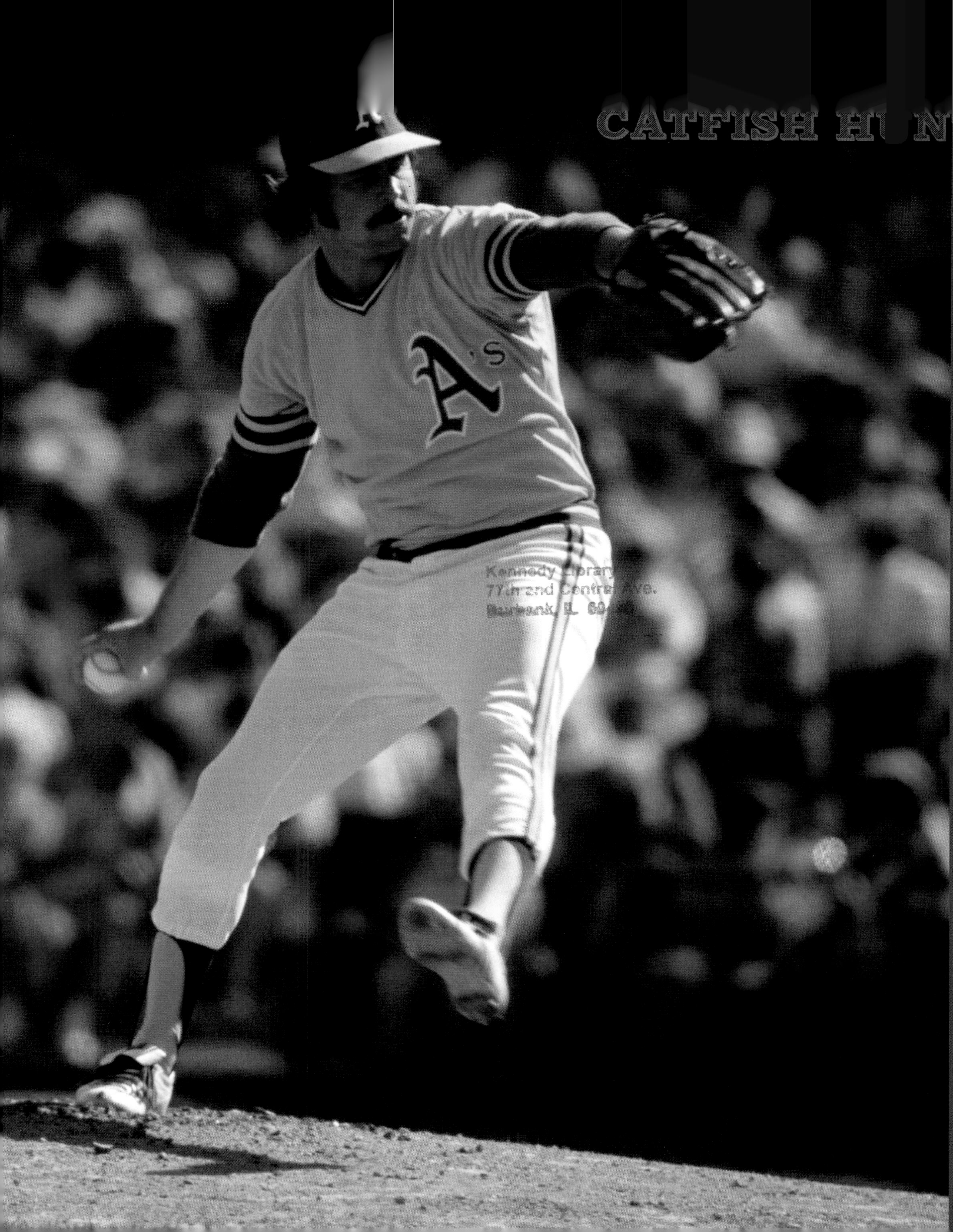

Mustachioed pitcher Rollie Fingers compiled a major-league record 341 saves before retiring in 1985.

(MVP) award and giving the A's their first three-peat. Asked by a reporter how one guided a team to victory, A's manager Alvin Dark responded, "A fellow has to have faith in God and Rollie Fingers in the bullpen."

The advent of free agency, along with Finley's unwillingness to pay his top players higher salaries, led to the loss of many A's stars in the late '70s, including Hunter and Jackson. Soon the once-mighty A's were sitting at the bottom of the AL West. Before the 1981 season, a frustrated Finley sold the team to San Francisco clothing manufacturer Walter Haas.

SHORTSTOP · MIGUEL TEJADA

Miguel Tejada, known as "Miggy" by his teammates, was drafted in 1993 at the age of 17. By the time he was 21, he had proven himself a crafty shortstop with a knack for making clutch plays and the muscle to slug home runs. In 2002, when his team needed him to step up during a tight division race, he did so by hitting .308 with 34 homers and helping the A's win their third straight AL West title. He also earned AL MVP honors that year, thanks in part to his game-winning hits in the 18th and 19th victories of Oakland's historic 20-game winning streak.

MIGUEL TEJADA
SHORTSTOP

OAKLAND ATHLETICS

STATS

Athletics seasons: 1997–2003

Height: 5-9

Weight: 215

- **2002 AL MVP**
- **24-game hitting streak (2002)**
- **4-time All-Star**
- **.286 career BA**

BILLY MARTIN

Billy Martin managed four different big-league teams to division titles but was frequently fired due to his temper.

BILLY BALL

Before Finley sold the team, he'd hired Billy Martin, who had managed the Yankees to world championship wins in 1977 and 1978. Martin introduced the A's to his unique style of play. "The A's aggressive style of hit and run, run and hit, and steal-steal-steal became known as 'Billy Ball,' and it attracted baseball fans all around the nation," noted sportswriter James Duplacey of Martin's new techniques.

It didn't take long for "Billy Ball" to produce results. In only one season, the bottom-dwelling A's turned into contenders. Outfielder Tony Armas slammed 35 home runs in 1980; left fielder Rickey Henderson stole 100 bases; and hurler Rick Langford put together a stretch of 22 complete games, the longest streak by any pitcher in team history.

As Billy Ball caught on, fans returned to Oakland's Alameda County Coliseum and watched their team reach second place in the AL West, finishing 83–79. The next year, the A's powered their way to a division title with their usual hitting, base stealing, and ironman pitching. They met the dominant Yankees and former teammate Reggie Jackson in the playoffs. The "Bronx Bombers" proved to be too much for the young A's team, defeating them three

LEFT FIELDER · RICKEY HENDERSON

Henderson wasn't nicknamed the "Man of Steal" for nothing. In all but one season, he led the AL in stolen bases from 1980 to 1991. In 1981, he snatched 100 bases. Two years later, he stole 130, breaking St. Louis Cardinals outfielder Lou Brock's single-season record of 118 thefts. In 1989, Henderson stole five bases in just one game against the Seattle Mariners, and on May 1, 1991, he became the first player to steal 1,000 bases. The muscular outfielder could also hit, collecting his 3,000th career base rap on October 7, 2001.

RICKEY HENDERSON
LEFT FIELDER

OAKLAND
ATHLETICS

STATS

Athletics seasons: 1979–84, 1989–93, 1994–95, 1998

Height: 5-10

Weight: 195

- **1,115 career RBI**

- **1,406 career stolen bases**

- **1990 AL MVP**

- **10-time All-Star**

games to zero. "The Yankees beat us," Martin said, "but nobody expected us to be here anyhow. We'll see you all next year."

But there wouldn't be a next year; three of the team's starting pitchers developed arm trouble in 1982, and Oakland dropped to a disappointing 68–94. Soon after, Martin was fired and returned to the Yankees.

RICKEY HENDERSON – The greatest base stealer of all time, Henderson had a most unique A's career. He spent 14 seasons in Oakland, but in four different stints, leaving for other teams and then returning. His knack for thievery made him a 10-time All-Star.

THE BASH BROTHERS

T hroughout the mid-1980s, the A's were a mediocre team and never came close to reaching the playoffs. But then two players arrived in 1986 and 1987 to turn things around. Outfielder Jose Canseco was the first to step into the limelight, winning Rookie of the Year honors in 1986 by notching 117 RBI and slamming 33 home runs. First baseman Mark McGwire was next, snatching the same award in 1987 after clubbing 49 home runs, the most ever by a major-league rookie. Canseco also hit 30 home runs that year, and the brawny duo quickly became known as the "Bash Brothers," not only for their hitting, but also for the forearm smash they used to celebrate each home run. The fad took off across America as baseball fans mimicked the forearm bash to celebrate terrific plays.

Canseco won the AL MVP award by a landslide in 1988, hitting 42 home runs, 27 of which tied a game or put the A's in the lead. After one home run against the California Angels, A's pitcher Dave Stewart said, "The shortstop could have hopped on that ball and taken a flight to New York." McGwire added 32 home runs, helping the A's post a league-best 104 victories. In the ALCS, the Bash Brothers combined for four home runs and batted over .300 to put away the Boston Red Sox, and in the World Series, Canseco hit a grand

MARK McGWIRE AND JOSE CANSECO – The Bash Brothers were Oakland teammates for seven seasons, and during that time they combined for three home run titles (McGwire in 1987 and Canseco in 1988 and 1991). The duo helped the A's win four division crowns.

slam, while McGwire slugged a game-winning home run in Game 3. Still, the Brothers' heroics weren't enough, and Oakland fell to the Los Angeles Dodgers four games to one.

Oakland bounced back with a return to the playoffs in 1989. This time, it was Rickey Henderson's turn to shine. The left fielder hit two home runs and stole eight bases to help the A's win another ALCS against the Red Sox. Henderson continued his hot streak in the World Series, batting .474 against Oakland's across-the-bay rivals, the San Francisco Giants, as the A's swept the Giants in four straight games for world championship number nine.

The Bash Brothers were at it again in 1990, hitting a total of 76 home runs to lift Oakland to another World Series. After winning 103 games and riding high on a 10-game postseason winning streak, the A's seemed ready to dominate the Cincinnati Reds. But it was the Reds who dominated, sweeping the A's in four games in a major upset.

Canseco and McGwire continued to frighten opponents with their long balls in 1991, but Oakland slipped to a disappointing fourth place. Then, in 1992, Canseco was traded to the Texas Rangers, splitting up the Bash Brothers. The next year, with McGwire plagued by injuries, the A's dropped to last place in the AL West, and team management traded away both Henderson and McGwire. Without these stars, Oakland vanished from the playoff picture for the rest of the '90s.

THE EARTHQUAKE GAME

The sister cities of Oakland and San Francisco met in the 1989 World Series in what was called the "Battle of the Bay." But that series would not be remembered for the A's dominance over the San Francisco Giants or the fact that the A's never trailed in any of the four games. What everyone remembered was the earthquake that struck in Game 3 of the series. On October 17, at 5:04 P.M., just as the pregame formalities got underway, an earthquake hit San Francisco's Candlestick Park. People shook in their seats, press boxes swayed, power went out, and TV broadcasts were disabled. Fortunately, no

one at the game was hurt, and the stadium sustained only minor damages. But outside, 67 people died, and billions of dollars' worth of property was damaged. San Francisco was left in shambles and its people in shock. Immediately, Baseball Commissioner Fay Vincent postponed the game. Some people wanted the series cancelled altogether, but after long talks, it was decided that the series would only be delayed until October 27. The 10-day gap was the longest in World Series history. In the end, the A's won four games to zero and dedicated the championship to the victims of the quake.

MIGUEL TEJADA

THE 20-GAME STREAK

Late in the summer of 2002, the Oakland Athletics went on an amazing 20-game winning streak. It was the longest streak in baseball history since the Chicago Cubs had won 21 in a row in 1935, and it was only 6 short of the record set by the New York Giants in 1916. But in August and September 2002, the A's wanted to do more—they wanted to break history. During those 20 games, A's shortstop Miguel Tejada hit a whopping .372, and it was because of his game-winning hits that they won games 18 and 19. In their 20th game, playing at home in front of 55,528 fans, the A's jumped out to an 11–0 lead by the third inning. It seemed as if it would be an easy win for Oakland, but the Kansas City Royals battled back, tying the A's in the top half of the ninth inning. Unwilling to lose the streak, Oakland pinch hitter Scott Hatteberg responded in the bottom of the ninth by swatting a game-ending home run that secured the 20th win. Two days later, however, the A's were shut out 6–0 by the Minnesota Twins, ending the historic run.

CENTER FIELDER · AL SIMMONS

Born as Aloys Szymanski to Polish immigrants, this Wisconsin native changed his name to Al Simmons after seeing a billboard advertisement for Al Simmons Tobacco. In each of his first 11 big-league seasons, Simmons knocked in at least 100 RBI and never batted below .300. He hit 307 career home runs and was a deadly clutch hitter. One game, after Simmons had badly hurt his knee, the A's were down 7–4 and the bases were loaded. Simmons was brought in to pinch-hit. He limped to the plate and, on the first pitch, smashed a grand slam to win the game.

STATS

Athleticss seasons: 1924–32, 1940–41, 1944

Height: 5-11

Weight: 190

- **.334 career BA**

- **1,827 career RBI**

- **3-time All-Star**

- **Baseball Hall of Fame inductee (1953)**

AL SIMMONS
CENTER FIELDER

OAKLAND
ATHLETICS

THE BIG THREE

The success the Oakland A's enjoyed from 2000 to 2004 can be attributed to a number of things, but one thing is for sure—it could not have been achieved without the stellar pitching of Barry Zito, Mark Mulder, and Tim Hudson, known as "The Big Three." The first of the three to start was Hudson, who arrived in 1999 and went 11–2 in his rookie season. In 2000, Mulder and Zito joined the rotation as Hudson recorded 20 wins and nearly won the Cy Young Award as the league's best pitcher. The next season was a breakout year for The Big Three, as they combined for a staggering 56 wins. In 2002, Zito was at the top of his game. The left-hander used a 90-mile-per-hour fastball and an excellent curveball (which was nicknamed "Captain Hook" or "Bert") to win 23 games, record a 2.75 ERA, notch 182 strikeouts, and finally bring the Cy Young Award to Oakland. The 2002 season marked the first time in 102 years that a team had three different 20-game winners under the age of 25 in consecutive seasons. The Big Three disbanded after the 2004 season when Hudson and Mulder were traded away.

A lanky lefty with masterful breaking pitches, Mark Mulder won 21 games in 2001, tops in the league.

MARK MULDER

ERIC CHAVEZ

The AL's best defensive third baseman, Eric Chavez won the Gold Glove award every year from 2001 to 2006.

NEW HOPE IN OAKLAND

There was reason for Bay area fans to hope again in 2000, as third baseman Eric Chavez and first baseman Jason Giambi combined for 69 home runs to boost the A's back into the playoffs. Oakland faced the New York Yankees in the AL Division Series (ALDS) and got off to a quick start by winning Game 1, but the Yankees bounced back to take the next two. On the verge of elimination, the A's responded with an 11–1 victory in Game 4, sending the series back to Oakland for the final game. Before the A's could get their first at bat, New York's "Bronx Bombers" had scored six runs in the first inning, and Oakland could not recover. The A's were beaten, but their spirits were high. "We had a great season," said outfielder Terrence Long. "We played like a championship team. We'll be back."

The A's were back, returning to the playoffs the next three years, carried by ace pitchers Tim Hudson, Barry Zito, and Mark Mulder, collectively known as "The Big Three." However, the A's were beaten three games to two in the ALDS every time, becoming the first team in baseball history to lose decisive playoff games four years in a row. Oakland took a gamble in 2004, allowing star shortstop Miguel Tejada to leave as a free agent and trusting

BARRY ZITO

Barry Zito was a durable starter famous for his looping curveball. He left Oakland before the 2007 season.

RIGHT FIELDER · REGGIE JACKSON

Reggie Jackson may have been the first baseball player to ever have a candy bar named after him (the Reggie Bar), but his more important name was "Mr. October," which he later earned for his pattern of postseason heroics. He was part of six AL pennant winners and five World Series championships throughout his career and assembled a .357 career batting average in World Series games. In Game 6 of the 1977 World Series, playing for the Yankees, Jackson hit three home runs on three pitches in three straight at bats. The slugger finished his career with 563 home runs.

REGGIE JACKSON
RIGHT FIELDER

OAKLAND
ATHLETICS

STATS

Athletics seasons: 1967–75, 1987

Height: 6-0

Weight: 200

• **4-time AL leader in HR**

• **1,702 career RBI**

• **14-time All-Star**

• **Baseball Hall of Fame inductee (1993)**

MANAGER · CONNIE MACK

Connie Mack began his baseball career as a catcher, but it wasn't until after he quit playing that he made his greatest mark. For 50 years, he was owner and manager of the Philadelphia Athletics. He commanded his players by wearing a business suit in the dugout and led his team to nine AL pennants and five victorious World Series. He holds the all-time record for most wins as manager—and most losses as well. Mack was a patient man who rarely confronted a player in front of other people and hardly ever raised his voice.

CONNIE MACK
MANAGER

OAKLAND
ATHLETICS

STATS

Athletics seasons as manager:
   1901–50

Height: 6-1

Weight: 150

Managerial Record: 3,731–3,948

World Series Championships: 1910,
   1911, 1913, 1929, 1930

untested Bobby Crosby to fill his shoes. The risk paid off, as Crosby hit 22 home runs and became the overwhelming choice for AL Rookie of the Year. Still, the team finished in second place that year and the next.

The 2006 A's featured many new faces, but by season's end, they had captured another AL West title. Veteran designated hitter Frank Thomas drove in 114 runs, pitcher Danny Haren won 14 games, and outfielder Nick Swisher slugged 35 homers. The A's swept the Minnesota Twins in the ALDS but were then swept themselves by the Detroit Tigers in the ALCS. Oakland then lost two key cogs as well when Zito and Thomas departed as free agents, leaving fans to hope that such players as Chavez, Swisher, Haren, and closer Huston Street would pick up the slack. "It's a new beginning, a new identity," said outfielder Milton Bradley. "A new brand of A's baseball."

The Oakland A's are a team with a long and legendary history of success from the days of Connie Mack, to the Bash Brothers, and beyond. Oakland's latest generation of stars does not have to look far to draw inspiration to continue the winning tradition that will one day ship a world championship back to the Port of Oakland.

INDEX

Alameda County Coliseum 31

All-Star Game 18

AL Championship Series 22, 24, 26, 34, 36, 47

AL Division Series 43, 47

AL pennants 6, 9, 11, 15, 16, 17, 46

AL Western Division championships 22, 24, 26, 29, 31, 47

Armas, Tony 31

Baker, Frank 12

Bando, Sal 22, 24

Baseball Hall of Fame 10, 13, 15, 17, 18, 39, 45

"Bash Brothers" 34, 36, 47

Bender, Charles "Chief" 9, 12

Bishop, Max 23

Bradley, Milton 47

Campaneris, Bert 22, 26

Canseco, Jose 34, 36

Chavez, Eric 43, 47

Cochrane, Mickey 13

Coombs, Jack 9

Cramer, Doc 17

Crosby, Bobby 47

Cy Young Award 40

Dark, Alvin 28

Dykes, Jimmy 16, 23

Earnshaw, George 15, 16, 17

Ehmke, Howard 16

Federal League 12

Fingers, Rollie 22, 26, 28

Finley, Charlie O. 20, 28, 31

Foxx, Jimmie 15, 16, 18

Giambi, Jason 43

Grove, Lefty 10, 13, 15, 16, 17, 19

Haas, Walter 28

Haren, Danny 47

Hatteberg, Scott 38

Henderson, Rickey 31, 32, 36

Hudson, Tim 40, 43

Hunter, Jim "Catfish" 22, 28

Indianapolis Indians 6

Jackson, Reggie 5, 22, 25, 26, 28, 45

Johnson, Arnold 20

Kansas City Athletics 20

  relocation to Oakland 20

Kansas City Municipal Stadium 20

Knowles, Darold 25

Langford, Rick 31

Long, Terrence 43

Mack, Connie 6, 11, 12, 15, 16, 17, 19, 20, 46, 47

major-league records 32, 34

Mangual, Angel 25

Marquez, Gonzalo 25

Martin, Billy 31, 33

McGwire, Mark 34, 36

Miller, Bing 16, 17

MVP award 5, 10, 13, 18, 26, 29, 32, 34

Mulder, Mark 40, 43

perfect games 22

Philadelphia Athletics 6, 9, 10, 11, 12, 13, 15, 16, 17, 18, 19, 20, 23, 39, 46

  relocation to Kansas City 20

Plank, Eddie 9, 12

Rookie of the Year award 34, 47

Rudi, Joe 25

Simmons, Al 16, 19, 39

Stewart, Dave 34

Street, Huston 47

Swisher, Nick 47

team records 17, 31

Tejada, Miguel 29, 38, 43

Tenace, Gene 5, 25, 26

Thomas, Frank 47

Western League 6

white elephant logo 11

world championships 5, 9, 12, 15, 16, 25, 26, 28, 36, 37, 46

World Series 5, 6, 9, 11, 12, 13, 15, 16, 17, 22, 25, 26, 28, 34, 36, 37, 45, 46

World Series earthquake (1989) 37

World Series records 5, 16, 25

Zito, Barry 40, 43, 47